What is a
PATKA?

This book is dedicated to those who work
to create a more accepting world.

And to the original Mohan,
the inspiration of this book
and so much more.

www.whatisapatka.com

What is a
PATKA?

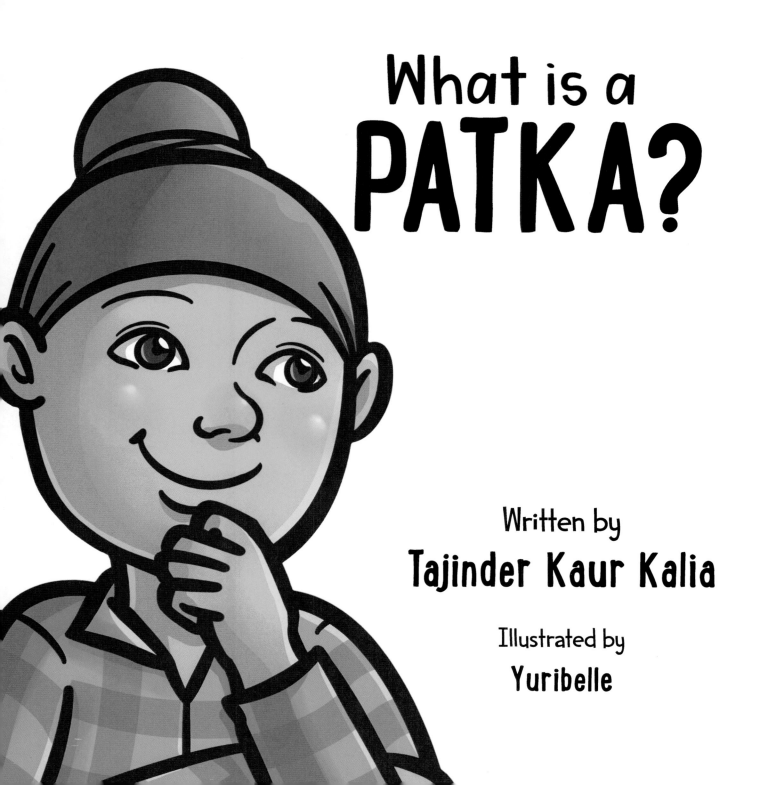

Written by
Tajinder Kaur Kalia

Illustrated by
Yuribelle

This is **Mohan**.

He lives in a house
in New York with
his Mom and Dad.

He likes to ride his bike,
eat French fries,
and play with his friends

Mohan is Sikh,
because his Mom and Dad are Sikhs!
Being Sikh means he
follows certain rules...

The first rule is that he must be kind
and help anyone who needs it.

He also can't cut his hair
he has to keep it long!

His Dad, his Mom, and
all the people in his family
keep their hair long too!

How does Mohan keep his long hair tidy while he plays?

He wears a **PATKA!**
A patka is a cloth square with strings at each corner.

Mohan's mom or dad combs his hair and ties the patka over his hair every morning.

This keeps his hair tidy.

It's important to remember
that his hair and patka should not
be touched – unless he gives **permission!**

Patkas come in many different colors and patterns!

Patkas can match with outfits and they can match with moods!

Mohan has many friends who wear patkas and many friends who **DON'T** wear patkas!

Looking different on the outside doesn't stop them from being friends!

Step One

Make sure the hair is neatly combed.

*Neater hair will make finishing the patka easier later on!

Step Two

Find the side of the patka without a sewn seam (there will only be one!) and position that over the forehead.

*It should be a straight line across the forehead. slightly above the eyebrows.

Step Three

Tie the corresponding ties at the base of the neck.

*Don't let the knot get too high...pull it down nice and low in the back. so that the whole patka doesn't ride up!
*This should be fairly tight... not to create red lines on the child's forehead. but tight enough to hold in that position. Too loose. and it will move and rub and be very uncomfortable!

patka

Step Four
Pull up one of the back 'flaps' – you will wrap it around the (now covered) hair knot.

Step Five
You will do the same thing with the other back flap.

(Note - it might be easy to have the child hold the string on the side of their head so you can use both hands to pull the flap around the hair)

Step Six
You should now have two strings at the top of the head that you can tie neatly and tuck into the ends.

ALL DONE! You should now have a tidy and comfortable patka!

DESIGN YOUR OWN PATKA!

CLASSROOM IDEAS

- Send the book into the teacher well before the presentation. This will give them a chance to review it, ask you questions, and get approval, if required.

- If you bring a snack, be sure to approve it with the teacher first (due to allergies/school policies).

- Ask your child if (s)he wants to play a part in the presentation - read the book, pass around the patkas or help choose the patkas to bring in. Allowing your child to 'own' part of the presentation will build confidence and give him/her the tools to answer questions on their own.

- Bring some patkas with varying colors and patterns and let the children pass them around - this will give them a chance to feel a patka without touching one while someone is wearing it.

- Bring copies of the coloring page! Each child can design their own patka.

- Consider donating a copy of What is a Patka? to your child's school library as a Vaisakhi gift.

- Have fun!!! Children are naturally curious, use that curiosity to foster discussion and learning. There are no bad questions!!